THERE'S A HAT FOR THAT!

A GIFT TO:

FROM:

DATE:

Exploring Careers That Fit You Best

There's a Hat for That!
© 2021 by Dr. Kevin J. Fleming

Published by Bolígrafo Books
An imprint of Grafo House Publishing
Guadalajara, Jalisco, Mexico / grafohouse.com
In association with Jaquith Creative
Bothell, Washington, USA / jaquithcreative.com

Words by Dr. Kevin J. Fleming
Cover and interior artwork by Iskar.

hardbound ISBN 978-1-949791-57-0
paperback ISBN 978-1-949791-58-7
ebook ISBN 978-1-949791-59-4

Library of Congress Control Number: 2021911021

Bulk discounts available for schools, public institutions, and events.
For more information or to contact the author, visit www.kevinjfleming.com

Printed in the United States of America
24 23 22 21   1 2 3 4

To Aria
You'll always be my little monkey.
Wearing my "dad hat" has been
my absolute favorite by far.

One day I will grow up,
but what will I be?

Will I find a job
with a hat just for me?

Perhaps I'll like words;
I could become a writer.
I'll report what I see
and make people's lives brighter.

Or maybe I'll turn out
to be strong and brave.
As a firefighter,
just think who I'll save!

My gift could be music.
I'll play in a band.
Singing and dancing
across every land.

Or I could want
to keep peace on the street.
I'll be an officer
"walking the beat."

Perhaps I will learn
I'm a very good cook.
I'll publish my recipes
in my own book.

I might be creative;
I'll learn a new trade.
Carpentry, welding;
I'll sell what I've made.

I could love design
and the way buildings rise.
As an architect, I'll make things
that stretch to the skies.

Maybe I'll find
that computers are fun.
I'll engineer robots
for everyone.

I might like questions
and asking, "But why?"
I'll invent something
no one thought to try.

I could love numbers
and getting things right.
I'll solve crazy problems
and do math all night.

Or I might find
that I want to feel free.
I'll start my own business
and I'll work for me!

Perhaps I'll love reptiles,
like big snakes and frogs.
I could be a vet,
healing birds, cats, and dogs.

There's a chance I'll love nature
and rivers and trees.

I'll be a park ranger
or take care of bees.

I could love the water
much more than the trees.
I'll captain a ship
and sail the high seas.

I may learn a language,
or two, three, or four.
I'll help people to
understand others more.

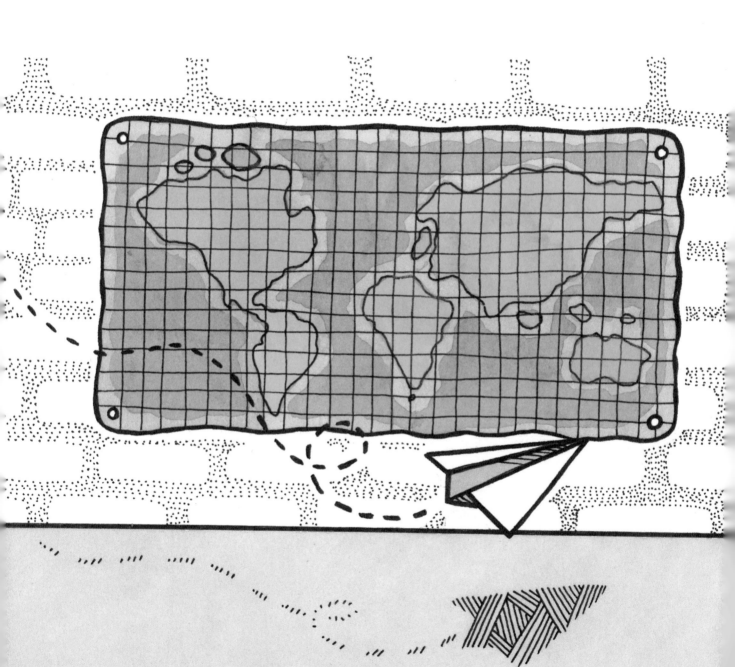

Maybe I'll love teaching
and helping kids learn.
I'll coach them to read,
each one taking a turn.

Maybe I'll like
making others feel great.
I'll do hair and makeup
for important dates.

I might like planning
for things far away.
I'll help invest money
for a rainy day.

There are so many jobs
to explore and to test.
With my natural skills,
I'll find which hat fits best.

Sometimes I may fail,
other times I'll succeed.
I'll learn something new
every time, guaranteed.

When I grow up one day,
what will I be?
I could be a parent
to a great kid like me!

Dear Parent,

Did you know that there are over 800 different occupations to choose from? All jobs can be categorized within sixteen different clusters to help make career exploration easy and fun.

Your child is probably already showing interests, abilities, gifts, and unfulfilled potential in many areas. As their unique personality continues to gravitate toward certain types of activities and careers, encourage play which explores all their options. Helping to find the alignment between your child's natural abilities and possible career choices is a fun journey that you can enjoy together!

At least one job from each cluster is used in this book as an example, but there are so many more careers to explore. Some hats will naturally fit your child better than others. Never stop exploring all the occupations for which your child may be a perfect fit.

For more career exploration information, tools, books, and videos, visit www.kevinjfleming.com.

CAREER CLUSTERS	SAMPLE OCCUPATIONS
Agriculture, Food & Natural Resources	Park Ranger, Beekeeper, Environmental Engineers, Soil Scientists, Water Resource Specialists
Architecture & Construction	Architect, Carpenters, Pipe Fitters, Cost Estimators, Solar Thermal Installers
Arts, Audio/Video Technology & Communications	Writer, Journalist, Musician, Agent/ Business Manager, Graphic Designer
Business Management & Administration	Entrepreneur, Customer Service Representative, Human Resources Manager, Fundraiser
Education & Training	Teacher, Archivist, Athletic Coach, Teacher Assistant, Interpreter/ Translator
Finance	Investor, Accountant, Bookkeeper, Loan Officer, Insurance Sales Agent, Personal Financial Advisor
Government & Public Administration	Police Officer, Military, Freight & Cargo Inspector, Urban and Regional Planner, Occupational Health Safety Technician
Health Science	Veterinarian, Medical Secretary, Phlebotomist, Dental Assistant, Acupuncturist

CAREER CLUSTERS	SAMPLE OCCUPATIONS
Hospitality & Tourism	Head Cooks, Executive Chefs, Travel Guides, Gaming Supervisors, Amusement Park Attendants
Human Services	Hairstylists and Cosmetologist, Personal Trainer, Loan Counselors, School Psychologists, Nannies
Information Technology	Computer Systems Engineer, Database Architect, Video Game Designer, Website Administrator, Computer User Support Specialist
Law, Public Safety, Corrections & Security	Firefighter, Paramedics, Forest Fire Inspector & Prevention Specialist, Court Reporter, Security Guard
Manufacturing	Carpenter, Welder, Machinist, Fire Alarm System Installer, Computer Numerically Controlled Machine Programmer
Marketing	Entrepreneur, Property Manager, Cashier, Real Estate Agent, Sales Representative
Science, Technology, Engineering & Mathematics	Mathematician, Inventor, Marine Engineer, Atmospheric and Space Scientist, Quality Control Analyst, Remote Sensing Technician
Transportation, Distribution & Logistics	Boat Captain, Supply Chain Technician, Bicycle Repairer, Airplane Pilot, Heavy and Tractor-Trailer Truck Driver

Author
Dr. Kevin Fleming

Dr. Kevin J. Fleming is an educator, speaker, entrepreneur, and recovering academic elitist. He is the producer of viral animation videos including "Success in the New Economy," author of educational bestseller *(Re)Defining the Goal*, and VP of Planning & Development at Norco College. Dr. Fleming is a leader in the national dialogue around eliminating the skills gap by giving learners knowledge, training, and abilities. He is a passionate advocate for students to equip their potential, enter the labor market with a competitive advantage, and find their purpose on purpose. Dr. Fleming is a proud eagle scout, husband, author, and member of Sigma Phi Epsilon fraternity, has earned five degrees, and has completed five marathons. But of all the hats he has worn, his favorite by far is "dad." Learn more at www.KevinJFleming.com.

Illustrator
Iskar

Oscar Olivares ("Iskar") was born and raised in Guadalajara, Mexico but has called many places home throughout his artistic journey. Since early childhood he has been drawing and creating characters, turning friends and people around him into stories and adventures. A love of vintage comics and illustration has been a constant inspiration in his work. Currently he is enjoying a career as an urban and contemporary artist, dividing his time between the streets of Los Angeles and Mexico.

Made in the USA
Middletown, DE
03 September 2021